Lee's surrender of the Army of Northern Virginia to Grant at Appomattox in April 1865. *Painting by Benjamin West Clinedinst, 1897.*

An Historical Walk *at the* Santa Maria Cemetery: American Civil War Veterans

By

Cindy Ransick
Santa Maria Valley Historical Society

Edited by Michael W. Farris

JANAWAY PUBLISHING
Santa Maria, California

Copyright © 2015, Santa Maria Valley Historical Society

ALL RIGHTS RESERVED.
No part of this publication may be reproduced, stored in a
retrieval system, or transmitted in any form or by any
means whatsoever, whether electronic, mechanical,
magnetic recording, or photocopying, without the
prior written approval of the Copyright holder
or Publisher, excepting brief quotations
for inclusion in book reviews.

Author: Cindy Ransick

Editor: Michael W. Farris

Published for Santa Maria Valley Historical Society

by:

Janaway Publishing, Inc.
732 Kelsey Ct.
Santa Maria, California 93454
(805) 925-1038
www.janawaygenealogy.com

2015

Library of Congress Control Number: 2015947695

ISBN: 978-1-59641-363-4

Copies of this book may be purchased from Santa Maria Valley Historical
Society, 616 S. Broadway, Santa Maria, CA 93454.
For more information, please write, or phone (805) 922-3130.

Made in the United States of America

Table of Contents

Overview 1
Mr. Lincoln and Santa Maria 3
Union Veterans of the War Between the States 5
Patrick Henry **Bartron** 7
    Pennsylvania
Ferdinand **Bauman** 8
    Kansas
James **Blakey** 9
    Artillery
John **Bundy** 10
    Indiana
Henry **Cain** 11
    Regular Army
Hiram Webster **Copeland** 12
    Rhode Island
Alvin Warner **Cox** 13
    Missouri
Edmund Luther **Criswell** 15
    Illinois
Moses Spenser **Davis** 16
    Veteran Reserve Corps
Rinaldo **Dodge** 17
    Wisconsin
Walter **Elliott** 19
    New York
Franklin F **Field** 21
    Connecticut
James Hamilton **Foulk** 22
    Infantry
Samuel Minor **Gale** 23
    Pensions
James **Hall** 24
    Michigan
John Allen **Haye** 25
    Animals of the Civil War
William Martin **Hite** 26
    Battlefield Medicine
Alden S. **Johnson** 27
    California
Benjamin Franklin **Lambert** 28
Santa Maria Cemetery 30
Cemetery Map 31
John P. **Litzenberg** 32
    28th Regiment, Pennsylvania Volunteers

John Luna **Marshall** 33
    Civil War Dead
John Curtis **May** 34
    Mechanics & Fusiliers Letter
Giles Ward **Mead** 35
Oliver Perry **Moore** 36
    Old Soldiers Home
Thomas L. **Morgan** 38
    Iowa
Ormond Pinkerton **Paulding** 39
William Vaughn **Powell** 41
Adolph **Pritchard** 42
    North Carolina Mountain Infantry
Alfred Wesley **Robinson** 43
    Union Civil War Veterans Headstones
William Wilson **Stilwell** 44
Antonio Nunes **Silva** 45
Robert G. **Stowe** 46
Jesse H. **Thornburgh** 47
    Drummer Boy
Joseph W. **Thornburgh** 48
George **Van Order** 49
M. Sibley **Willson** 50
    Goober Peas: A Confederate Campfire Song
Joseph Henry **Wilson** 51
    US Navy Civil War
Riner **Yelkin** 52
    Andersonville Prison
Civil War Generals Killed by "Friendly Fire" 53
Confederate States of America Veterans 55
Lion of Lucerne: Oakland Cemetery, Atlanta, GA 56
Woman's Relief Corps 57
John Harrison **Haydon** 58
    Confederate Pension Act
    The Southern Cross of Honor
William S. **Lawrence** 59
    Camp of Instruction
William T. **Miles** 60
    Virginia Sharpshooters
    Fort Donelson
George A. **Miller** 61
    2nd Battalion Alabama Light Artillery
Grand Army of the Republic 62
Foote Post No. 89, G.A.R. Santa Maria 63
Bibliography 64
Acknowledgements 65

Overview

The American Civil War, a tragic period in the history of the United States, overshadows a productive era in our history. Only 85 years after the American Revolution, the Civil War set brother against brother, inciting intrastate wars and stymying our country's development. Twenty-three states set poised for battle, with territories gambling their prosperity, betting their futures on the advantages or disadvantages admission as a free-soil or slave state might bring to bear to future generations.

123rd Ohio Volunteer Infantry Color Guard

Once again Americans were fighting for their ideals. A vast gulf lay between the industrial north and the agricultural south. So few years from their revolutionary ancestors, the southern states decided to create their own country separate from the United States government. President Abraham Lincoln could not let this action stand. If force must be used, then so be it; the country must not be divided. Representing one historical perspective and provoking a key moment in our national history, the powerful strife of the 1860s still pervades our culture. Even today, the debate over the issues that drew the United States into a war against itself are still challenged and contested by those who read and study history. It is insinuated that to attribute the war to "states' rights" ignores the obvious injustice and intolerance of slavery that raged in 1860 America.

The only agreement on the tragedy that is the Civil War was that it was highly politically motivated and manipulated by all parties. The outcome was the death of slavery and a reconstruction period that produced vast wealth for a select minority of men. The development of medicine, railroads, steel, and manufacturing rushed the re-united states into an industrial age. It freed the slave but did little for rights for Black Americans.

The human loss was devastating. Nearly as many men died in military prisons during the Civil War as were killed in the whole of the Vietnam War. Hundreds of thousands died of disease. An estimated 620,000 men died in the line of duty, roughly 2% of the population.

The pages that follow are meant as a tribute to those who served. For whatever the political, religious, or human rights issues that precipitated

the Civil War, it is important to remember those who willingly committed themselves to service of their ideals. We offer no judgement. We acknowledge their service and sacrifice.

Cindy Ransick
Curator
Santa Maria Valley Historical Museum

Mr. Lincoln and Santa Maria

It would be untrue to state that had President Lincoln not been assassinated in 1865, he would have undoubtedly have retired in Santa Maria. However, using Lincoln's "historical reputation" we can speculate on what might have happened.

In October of 2012 a collection of three scrapbooks were discovered in the Santa Maria Valley Historical Museum. They belonged to Laura Rose Burnham, who died in Santa Maria in 1959, and were donated by her widower, Harold Ashley Burnham in the 1980s. Laura Rose was Leonard Swett's only direct decedent, his granddaughter. The next question is, "who is Leonard Swett?"

Our story begins in Bloomington, Illinois, when a young Illinois lawyer named Leonard Swett became a close friend of Judge David Davis. Swett's travels took him through the Eighth Judicial District in the years between 1850 and 1860. He was on the same footpath as another aspiring Illinois lawyer, Abraham Lincoln. Swett met Lincoln, often practiced in the same courts, and began a warm personal friendship. Their admiration, each man for the other, was genuine.

Judge Davis and Mr. Swett both venerated Lincoln. They saw that he was the man the Nation needed, and it was their efforts which led to Lincoln's nomination. Mr. Swett was a prime motivator in this and was a controlling influence in planning and executing the remarkable campaign that resulted in Lincoln's eventual nomination and ultimate election.

With Lincoln's successful move to the Executive Mansion, came the opportunities to reward his staunchest supporters. Swett

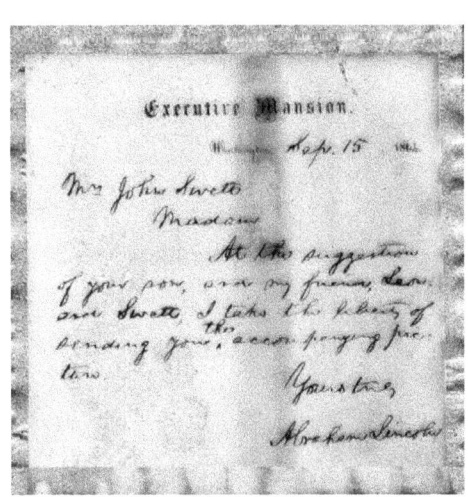

Letter to Mrs.Swett from President Lincoln sent with the photograph below.

reportedly told Lincoln he would enjoy a chance to have something that would pay, as he had had little time to practice law. Lincoln acted on the suggestion and secured him the control of the great suit in which the California Quicksilver Mining Company and the great (New) Almaden mine were involved. Mr. Swett came back from California with a fee of $104,000.

Swett also returned with great stories of the west. One can speculate that these two friends talked of a less stressful period of time, when after the presidency, they might advance their personal fortunes.

It is only speculation. There is only one fact in evidence, Leonard Swett's granddaughter was living in Guadalupe in 1945 and in Santa Maria by 1959. Would her famous grandfather and his friend Lincoln have found their way to California if Lincoln had not been assassinated?

Of course, we will never know. The Museum has hundreds of letters written between Leonard Swett and the many personalities of the American Civil War. The correspondence is on display during the month of April most years. The letters begin in 1860 and continue through the 1880s.

**The President and Todd Lincoln
Photograph sent to Mrs. Swett.**

Union Veterans

of

The War Between the States

The last Union veteran,
Albert Henry Woolson,
died in 1956 at age 109.

Bartron, Patrick Henry
Company K, 149th Pennsylvania Infantry
Grave #10   Lot #51
Born: April 19, 1842. Died: February 1, 1920.

 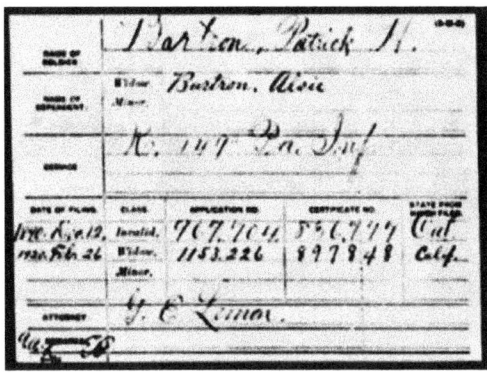

Patrick Henry Bartron claimed to be 21 years old when he enlisted as a private in Potter County, Pennsylvania, on August 16, 1862. He was mustered into Company K, 149th Pennsylvania Infantry, "the Bucktails," on August 26, 1862. Private H.Bartron was mustered out at Elmira, New York, on June 24, 1865. After the war, he went to Wisconsin where he married Alsia Anna Dodge at Pine Valley, Clark County, on February 1, 1871, then returned to Pennsylvania. He went to California in 1878 and was a resident at Mussel Slough, Tulare County, by 1880 (1880 US Census). He had settled at Santa Maria, Santa Barbara County, by 1883. He was a member of Santa Maria's Foote Post, No. 89, Grand Army of the Republic (1886 California Dept., G.A.R., Great Register). Bartron remained at Santa Maria until his death (1900, 1910 US census).

Pennsylvania

The Commonwealth of Pennsylvania played a critical role in the Union, providing military manpower, equipment, and leadership to the Union. Pennsylvania raised over 360,000 soldiers. Pennsylvania also served as a major source of artillery guns, small arms, ammunition, armor for the ironclad United States Navy gunboats, and food supplies.

The bloodiest battle of the war was fought at Gettysburg. Numerous smaller engagements were also fought in Pennsylvania during the 1863 Gettysburg Campaign and during an 1864 cavalry raid that culminated in the burning of much of Chambersburg, Pennsylvania. The industrial town of York, Pennsylvania, was the largest city in the North to be occupied by the Confederate States Army during the Civil War.

Bauman, Ferdinand
Company C, 23rd Kansas Militia Infantry
Grave #10   Lot #110
Born: January 8, 1846. Died: January 29, 1926.

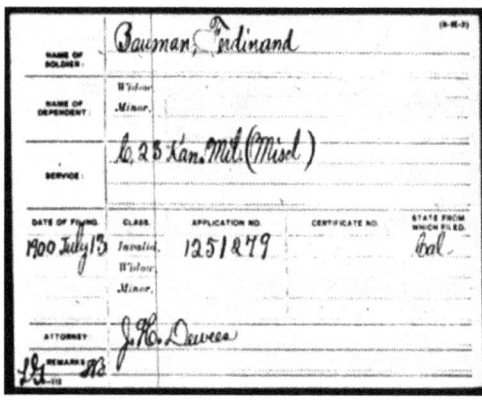

Kansas

Bleeding Kansas, a reference created by Republican Horace Greeley, editor of the New York Tribune, was so termed based on a series of violent political confrontations in the United States involving anti-slavery and pro-slavery elements that took place in the Kansas Territory and the neighboring towns of the state of Missouri between 1854 and 1861. The Kansas–Nebraska Act of 1854 called for "popular sovereignty," the decision about slavery was to be made by the settlers. It would be decided by votes, not politics. At the heart of the conflict was the question of whether Kansas would allow or outlaw slavery and thus enter the Union as a slave state or a free state. Pro-slavery forces said every settler had the right to bring his own property, including slaves, into the territory. Anti-slavery, "free soil," forces said the rich slaveholders would buy up all the good farmland and work them with black slaves, leaving little or no opportunity for non-slaveholders. Bleeding Kansas was a proxy war between anti-slavery forces in the North and pro-slavery forces from the South over the issue of slavery in the United States. Violence erupted indicating that compromise was unlikely and thus it portended the Civil War.

Blakey, James
9th Independent Battery, Wisconsin Light Artillery
Grave #6   Lot #15
Born: unknown. Died: unknown.

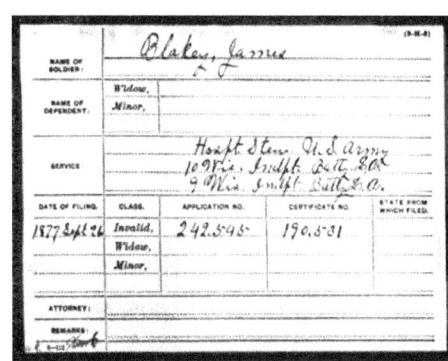

James Blakey enlisted as a private at New Lisbon, Wisconsin, on November 27, 1861. He was mustered out on December 9, 1863. He was a hospital steward. After the war he settled in California and was a member of Santa Maria's Foote Post, No. 89, Grand Army of the Republic (G.A.R.).

Artillery

Artillery was the official term for those batteries assigned to operate in the field with either infantry or cavalry; commonly called **Light Artillery**, although there is nothing light about them. Standard field pieces included the Parrott Rifles, 3-inch Ordnance Rifles, and the "Napoleon." Early on, the Union artillery eased its logistics burden by eliminating the older pieces almost entirely and relying on the rifled guns and Napoleons. By the end of the war, the Parrotts were themselves being phased out in favor of the lighter, safer, and more accurate Ordnance Rifles.

> Known for its reliability and accuracy, the 3-inch Ordnance Rifle was fielded by the artillery branches of both armies. Crafted from hammer-welded, machined iron the Ordnance Rifle typically fired 8 or 9 pound shells, as well as solid shot, case, and canister.

Bundy, John
Company A, 137th Indiana Infantry
Grave #2   Lot #102
Born: unknown. Died: January 19, 1908.

John Bundy was the son of Thomas D. Bundy and Mary Bogue. John was a resident of Howard County, Indiana, when he enlisted for 100 days on May 26, 1864, as a private. He was mustered into Co. A, 137th Indiana Infantry. Private Bundy was mustered out at Indianapolis, Indiana, September 21, 1864. After the war, he married Mary Catherine (maiden name unknown) in Indiana and settled at Jackson in Howard County where their son, Lewis Bundy, was born. John filed for a Civil War veteran's pension in Indiana on September 18, 1890. Sometime thereafter they relocated to Santa Maria, California, where John died on January 18, 1908. After John's death, Mary filed for a Civil War widow's pension at Santa Maria on February 11, 1908.

Indiana

In spite of significant antiwar activity in Indiana and southern Indiana's ancestral ties to the southern United States, it was a mainstay of the Union war effort. Residents of Indiana, called Hoosiers, served in every major engagement of the war and in almost every engagement, minor or otherwise, in the western theater. Agriculturally rich, Indiana contained the fifth-highest population in the Union and sixth-highest of all states. During the course of the war, Indiana contributed approximately 210,000 soldiers and millions of dollars in horses, food and supplies to the Union Army.

Cain, Henry
Regular Army
U S Army 2nd & 3rd Light Artillery Battery
Grave #6   Lot #300
Born: unknown. Died: January 19, 1908.

Henry Cain enlisted, at San Francisco, California, as a private, on October 24, 1859, in the U S Army 2nd and 3rd Light Artillery Battery. He served at Alcatraz Island and was discharged there on July 23, 1867.

Regular Army

The Regular Army of the United States was and is the successor to the Continental Army as the permanent, professional military establishment. Even today, the professional core of the United States Army continues to be called the Regular Army. From the time of the American Revolution until after the Spanish–American War, the small Regular Army of the United States was supported by State militias and volunteer regiments organized by States but thereafter controlled by federal authorities and generals in time of war. These volunteer regiments came to be called United States Volunteers (USV) in contrast to the Regular United States Army (USA). During the American Civil War, about 97% of the Union Army was United States Volunteers. Today, the term Regular Army refers to the full-time active component of the United States Army, as differentiated from the Army Reserve and the Army National Guard.

Copeland, Hiram Webster
1st Rhode Island Cavalry & 12 Massachusetts Infantry
Grave #2   Lot #83
Born: 1837. Died: January 1888.

First Rhode Island

Hiram Webster Copland enlisted in Company F, Massachusetts 12th Infantry Regiment on June 26, 1861. He was mustered out on January 8, 1862. His occupation was listed as clerk before the war. Committed Suicide at age 51 over not receiving his Civil War pension. Why he had problems is undetermined as his service is well documented. However, the 1862 statute that provided pensions was the foundation of the Federal pension system until the 1890s. It stipulated that only those soldiers whose disability was "incurred as a direct consequence of...Military duty" or developed after combat "from causes which can be directly traced to injuries received or diseases contacted while in military service" could collect pension benefits. The amount of each pension depended upon the veteran's military rank and level of disability. Pensions given to widows, orphans, and other dependents of deceased soldiers were always figured at the rate of total disability according to the military rank of their deceased husband or father. By 1873 widows could also receive extra benefits for each dependent child in their care.

Rhode Island

The state of **Rhode Island** during the American Civil War, as with all of New England, remained loyal to the Union. Rhode Island furnished 25,236 fighting men to the Union Army, of which 1,685 died. Rhode Island, along with the other northern states, used its industrial infrastructure to supply the Union Army with war implements.

Cox, Alvin Warner
Company M, Missouri 1st Cavalry Regiment
Grave #6   Lot #92
Born: June 4, 1863. Died: December 18, 1922.

Missouri

Missouri was a border state during the American Civil War. Missouri sent enlisted men, generals, armies and supplies to both sides; had its star on both flags and had separate governments representing each side. It endured a neighbor-against-neighbor intrastate war within the larger national war.

By the end, Missouri had supplied nearly 110,000 troops to the Union and at least 30,000 troops to the Confederate Army. There were battles and skirmishes in all areas of the state, from the Iowa and Illinois border in the northeast to the edge of the state in the southeast and southwest on the Arkansas border. Counting minor engagements, actions and skirmishes, Missouri saw over 1,200 individual clashes. Only Virginia and Tennessee participated in more clashes than Missouri in the number of fights within its borders.

Missouri Confederate Flag

Missouri was initially settled by Southerners coming up the Mississippi and Missouri Rivers. Many brought a few slaves. Missouri entered the Union in 1821 as a slave state following the Missouri Compromise of 1820, in which Congress agreed that no other territory north of 36°30' (Missouri's southern border with Arkansas) could enter the Union as a slave state. Maine entered the Union as a free state in the compromise to balance Missouri entrance as a slave state.

Criswell, Edmund Luther
Company G, 73rd Regiment Illinois Infantry
Unmarked Grave #1   Lot #83
Born: unknown. Died: 1890.

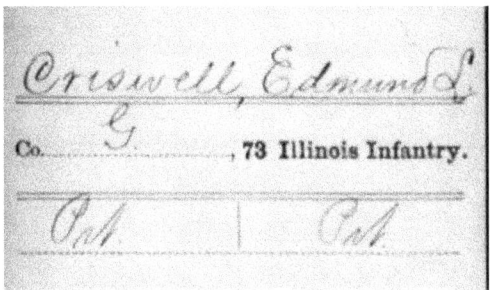

Illinois

During the Civil War, 256,297 Illinoisans served in the Union army. The state mustered 150 infantry regiments, which were numbered from the 7th Illinois to the 156th Illinois. Seventeen cavalry regiments were also mustered, as well as two light artillery regiments. Due to enthusiastic recruiting rallies and high response to voluntary calls to arms, the military draft was hardly used in Chicago, but was a factor in supplying manpower to Illinois regiments late in the war in other regions of the state.

Camp Douglas, located near Chicago, was one of the largest training camps for these troops, as well as Camp Butler near Springfield. Both served as leading prisoner-of-war camps for captive Confederates. Another significant POW camp was located at Rock Island. Several thousand Confederates died while in custody in Illinois prison camps and are buried in a series of nearby cemeteries.

There were no Civil War battles fought in Illinois.

Davis, Moses Spencer
7th Veterans Reserve Corps & Company K, 55th Illinois Infantry
Grave #6   Lot #143
Born: 1821. Died: 1895.

Veteran Reserve Corps

The Veteran Reserve Corps, originally the Invalid Corps, was a military reserve organization created within the Union Army during the American Civil War to allow partially disabled or otherwise infirmed soldiers to perform light duty, freeing all able-bodied soldiers to fight on the front lines.

Four members from Company F of the Fourteenth Veteran Reserves conducted the execution of the four conspirators linked to the assassination of Abraham Lincoln on July 7, 1865, at Fort McNair in Washington, D.C. They knocked out the post that released the platform that hanged Mary Surratt, Lewis Powell, David Herold, and George Atzerodt.

Dodge, Rinaldo
Company B, 47th Wisconsin Infantry
Grave #3   Lot #168
Born: May 15, 1847. Died: March 1, 1922.

 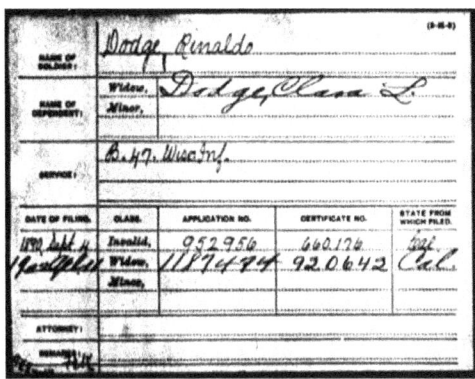

Rinaldo Dodge was the son of John Ellison Dodge and Ann Wadsworth Hutchins. He was living with his parents at Mendon, Michigan, in the United States in 1850. By 1860 he was living with his parents at Sodus, Berrien County, Michigan. He had moved to Wisconsin by 1864. During the Civil War he enlisted as a corporal at Madison, Wisconsin, on January 30, 1865, and was mustered into Company B, 47th Wisconsin Infantry. Corporal Dodge was mustered out at Nashville, Tennessee, on September 4, 1865. After the war he returned to Wisconsin and by 1870 was living in Lincoln, Eau Claire County. Sometime thereafter he relocated to California where he married Clara Lenora Cheadle at Hanford, Tulare County, on April 20, 1876. They were living at Mussel Slough, Tulare County, by 1880. By September 1880 the family had moved to Santa Barbara County and by 1885 they were living at Arroyo Grande, San Luis Obispo County. Rinaldo was a member of Santa Maria's Foote Post, No. 89, Grand Army of the Republic, by 1886 and lived in Santa Maria until at least 1889. Rinaldo had returned to Arroyo Grande by 1892, where he registered to vote. He was still at Arroyo Grande in 1900. By 1910 he had returned to Santa Maria, where he remained until he died.

Wisconsin

Wisconsin raised 91,379 soldiers for the North, which were organized into 53 infantry regiments, 4 cavalry regiments, a company of Berdan's sharpshooters, 13 light artillery batteries and 1 unit of heavy artillery. Most of the Wisconsin troops served in the Western Theater, although several regiments served in eastern armies, including three regiments within the famed Iron Brigade. 3,794 were killed in action or mortally wounded, 8,022 died of disease, and 400 were killed in accidents. The total mortality was 12,216 men, about 13.4 percent of total Wisconsin enlistments.

Nearly 1-in-9 Wisconsin residents served in the armed forces. Wisconsin was the only state to organize replacements for troops that had already been fielded, leading northern generals to prefer having some regiments from Wisconsin under their command whenever possible.

A number of Wisconsin regiments were distinguished, including three that served in the celebrated Iron Brigade: the 2nd Wisconsin, 6th Wisconsin, and 7th Wisconsin. They suffered severe casualties at the Battle of Gettysburg in July 1863. The 8th Wisconsin, another hard-fighting regiment, was often accompanied into battle by its mascot, Old Abe, a bald eagle.

Elliott, Walter
Company C, 20th New York Infantry
Grave #10   Lot #154
Born: December 24, 1840. Died: January 8, 1910.

Walter Elliot, Deputy Assessor of the Santa Barbara County, is among the citizens of Santa Maria who has shown the gift for successfully maintaining positions of trust from his townsmen. Born in Scotland in 1846, he is possessed of the strong reliant traits of his original countrymen. Elliot immigrated to the United States at the age of fifteen and settled in New York. He enlisted to fight in the Civil War as a private at Norwich, on September 1, 1864 with Company C, 20th New York Infantry. Elliot was discharged in the city of Richmond, June 17, 1865. After the war, Elliot lived briefly in New York and Illinois. In March of

1868, he came to California to see what opportunities he might engage in for the future. He traveled the state deciding upon a ranch fifteen miles east of San Jose where he farmed until November 1875. He then moved to Santa Maria district and ranched until 1891, at which time he moved into town. That same year he was elected county supervisor of the fifth district and served for eight years. Over the next ten years, Elliot served as deputy county assessor. It was reported of him that he repeatedly demonstrated that his service in all ways consulted the general good of the community, and that he regards public office as a means to further the general development, rather than an opportunity for personal aggrandizement. He is a member a member of the fraternity of the Masonic order and of the Knights of Pythias, and he is a past commander of the Grand Army of the Republic (G.A.R.).

New York

New York was the most populous state in the Union during the Civil War, and provided more troops to the Union Army than any other state. New York provided 400,000-460,000 men during the war, nearly 21% of all the men in the state and more than half of those under the age of 30.

Field, Franklin F.
Company A, 15th Regiment, Connecticut Infantry
Grave #2   Lot #134
Born: 1829. Died: 1891.

Connecticut

Connecticut residents such as Leonard Bacon, Simeon Baldwin, Horace Bushnell, Prudence Crandall, Jonathan Edwards (the younger) and Harriet Beecher Stowe, were active in the abolitionist movement. Connecticut towns such as Farmington and Middletown were stops along the Underground Railroad. Slavery in Connecticut had been gradually phased out in 1797 with less than 100 slaves in Connecticut by 1820; slavery was not completely outlawed until 1848.

The state, along with the rest of New England, had voted for Republican presidential candidate John C. Frémont in the 1856 presidential election, giving all 6 electoral votes. Santa Marian's will recognize his name readily as "The Pathfinder." The Republicans opposed the extension of slavery into the territories, and Connecticut residents embraced their slogan "Free speech, free press, free soil, free men, Frémont and victory!" Four years later, once again Connecticut favored the Republican candidate, this time Illinois lawyer Abraham Lincoln.

Foulk, James Hamilton
Company A, 149th Indiana Infantry
Grave #2   Lot #376
Born: January 28, 1840. Died: November 7, 1927.

James Hamilton Foulk enlisted in Company A, Indiana 149th Infantry Regiment on Jan 11, 1865. He was mustered out on September 27, 1865, at Nashville, Tennessee.

Infantry

Civil War **infantrymen**, both Union and Confederate, carried .58 or .577 caliber rifle-muskets. The rifle-musket was first manufactured in the United States in 1855 and quickly replaced earlier smoothbore weapons. The rifling, or spiral grooves, etched inside the gun's barrel increased the accuracy, by spinning and stabilizing the bullet as it sped toward the target. The trained marksman could hit targets at 800 yards. An average shot could expect to strike the mark at 250 yards. These rifle-muskets were chiefly percussion weapons. Pulling the trigger caused the hammer to strike a small metal cap. A charge of fulminate of mercury inside the cap would explode igniting the gunpowder charge in the barrel. The force of the gunpowder explosion drove the bullet down the barrel. The metal cap was tiny, about the size of a pencil eraser, and had to be set into place by hand each time the musket was fired. Soldiers had to follow nine steps to load and fire a single bullet from a muzzle-loading gun. Five steps were required to fire a breech-loading weapon. Rifle-muskets weighed between six and ten pounds, and many were designed to fit a bayonet on the end of the barrel. With so many steps to prepare to fire upon an advancing enemy, the bayonet was a useful and expedient weapon.

Gale, Samuel Minor
Co. E and C, 2nd Missouri State Militia Cavalry
Grave #1   Lot #152
Born: November 11, 1842. Died: June 11, 1887.

Samuel Minor Gale was the son of John Wesley Gale, Jr., and Rebecca McCrary. Samuel was living with his parents on the family farm outside Vernon, Van Buren County, Iowa, in October 1850 (1850 US Census). He was living with his widowed mother in Appanoose County, Iowa, in June 1860 (1860 US Census). During the Civil War he enlisted as a private on February 1, 1862, and was mustered into Company E, 2nd Missouri State Militia Cavalry. He was later transferred to Company C. Samuel married Elvira Delphine Robinson in Schuyler County, Missouri, on June 9, 1863. After the war Samuel moved to California where he had a farm in Tulare County from at least 1870 until 1880. He

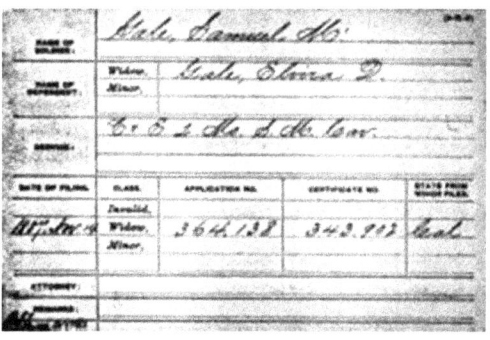

had moved to Santa Maria by 1885, where he was a member of Foote Post, No. 89, Grand Army of the Republic (G.A.R.). After his death Elvira filed for a Civil War widow's pension at Santa Maria on November 14, 1887, and received application No. 364,138 and certificate No. 343,902.

Pensions

After the Revolutionary War, the United States government began administering a limited pension system to soldiers wounded during active military service or veterans and their widows pleading desperate or dire poverty. The early U.S. military pension system was minuscule compared to what it became as a result of the Civil War.

Hall, James (Sgt.)
8th Michigan Calvary
Grave #11   Lot #348
Born: August 14, 1841. Died: October 31, 1927.

Michigan

Michigan was a long way from the combat theaters of the war yet supplied a large number of troops and several generals, including George Armstrong Custer. When, at the beginning of the war, Michigan was asked to supply four regiments, Governor Austin Blair sent seven. Upon the arrival of Michigan's first volunteers, President Abraham Lincoln was prompted to remark, "Thank God for Michigan."

Approximately 90,000 Michigan men, nearly a quarter of the state's male population in 1860, served in the war. In addition to the approximately 600 men who joined the Union Navy, Michigan raised 34 regiments of infantry volunteers, one regiment of sharpshooters, eleven cavalry regiments, one engineer regiment, and numerous small independent units.

Haye, John Allen
Company F, 78th Illinois Infantry
Grave #3   Lot #164
Born: August 16, 1844. Died: April 27, 1917.

Animals of the Civil War

Animals adopted as mascots during the Civil War enjoyed the attention and devotion of entire regiments but provided something even more important to the men who claimed them: comfort and joy during a turbulent time.

Dogs were the most popular army mascots during the Civil War. Man's best friend, indeed, they were valued for the companionship they provided and the fact that most dogs could be trained to help forage for food, carry supplies, or even search for dead and wounded soldiers.

Bears were also popular mascots. Both Wisconsin and Minnesota boasted brigades who had bears in their ranks. When Union forces took West Liberty, Kentucky in 1861, the list of captured included 52 horses, 10 mules and one large bear.

Other regiments included hens, roosters, badgers, squirrels, raccoons, wildcats, and even pigs as mascots.

Hite, William Martin
Company K, 118th Indiana Infantry
Grave #1   Lot #130
Born: April 23, 1844. Died: June 16, 1916.

Battlefield Medicine

Union Army Major Dr. Jonathan Letterman is noted as the "Father of Battlefield Medicine" for his Civil War innovations. He realized that organizing the Medical Corps was a key component for wounded survival. The state of the battlefield after the fighting ended weighed heavily on both sides. In the beginning soldiers might lie for days on a field, waiting to be discovered and unable to advance or retreat with their army. The suffering of the wounded was compounded by the time it took for them to be recovered by either side and treated.

Before the war, medical supplies were handled by regular quartermaster wagons. This meant that medical supplies competed for a space with "beans and bullets." In 1862, Major (Dr.) Letterman began to create an ambulance corps and three tiers of field hospitals: at the battlefield for simple wound dressing, nearby for emergency surgery, and behind the lines for long term care and recovery. And while many doctors didn't understand what "germs" were, they noticed soldiers did better with clean sheets, fresh air, and sunlight. Military medicine was forever influenced across the world by Letterman's observations and innovations. In March of 1864, his system was officially adopted for the U.S. Army by an Act of Congress.

Johnson, Alden S.
Company A, 8th California Infantry
Grave #1   Lot # 227
Born: December 16, 1832. Died: July 7, 1906.

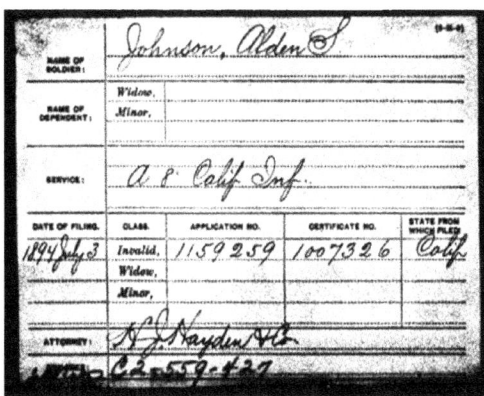

California

At one point California was to enter the Union as two states. The northern one would be a Free State called California and the southern one would be a territory which was to immediately become a Slave State called Colorado. This would maintain the balance of power in the Senate between the Northern Free States and the Southern Slave States. When California entered the Union as one Free State, the South saw the balance of power that they had so tenaciously hung onto in the Senate disappear. Southerners were extremely upset and many people feel that the entrance of California into the Union marks the real beginning of the Civil War.

Lambert, Benjamin Franklin
Company I, 18th Iowa Regiment
Grave #6   Lot #202
Born: July 4, 1839. Died: August 22, 1904.

Benjamin Franklin Lambert enlisted in Company I, Iowa 18th Infantry Regiment on August 06, 1862. He was mustered out on July 20, 1865 at Little Rock, Arkansas.

Benjamin Franklin Lambert enlisted on the first day. For this reason the details of the unit give a specific picture of his service. His regiment was mustered in Aug 5, 6 and 7, 1862. It moved to Springfield via St. Louis and Sedalia, joined the Army of the Southwest under Schofield and marched through Missouri into Arkansas. Returning to Springfield, it formed a part of the garrison there during the winter.

The following description of the regiment's activities through the summer 1865 is provided in the book *The Union Army: A History of Military Affairs in the Loyal States, 1861-65 -- Records of the Regiments in the Union Army – Cyclopedia of Battles – Memoirs of Commanders and Soldiers,* Volume 4:

> On Jan. 8, 1863, Marmaduke's forces, numbering over 5,000 men, attacked the garrison. The fight commenced about noon and continued with varying success until almost night, the enemy gaining ground at

times only to lose it by some daring charge, the tide being turned just before dark by the coming up of five companies of the 18th, which had been stationed at an outpost. They entered into the fight with such energy that the enemy was driven into a stockade at the outskirts of town and declined to give battle the following day, having lost more than 200 killed and wounded. The loss of the regiment was 56 killed and wounded and the loss to the entire Union force was about 200.

The regiment remained at Springfield about a year. Col. Edwards assumed command of the post in April, and in the fall was in temporary command of the district of southwestern Missouri, and later in command of his regiment, which formed part of the force that made Shelby throw aside his artillery and much of his baggage to escape his pursuers. Reaching Fort Smith, Arkansas, on Oct. 30, the regiment was assigned to garrison duty and spent the winter there with Col. Edwards being placed in command of the post. In March 1864, the regiment moved with Steele's forces to Arkadelphia, Col. Edwards being in command of the brigade to which the 18th was assigned. The command joined Thayer's forces at Elkin's ferry, the entire command then moved to Camden.

It was engaged at Prairie d'Ane and at Moscow, where Edwards' brigade stood the brunt of the attack and on being reinforced drove the enemy for several miles. After some ten days at Camden, the regiment engaged in a severe battle. With one section of the 2nd Indiana Battery, it was sent to reinforce Col. Williams of the 1st Kansas Colored Regiment, guarding a forage train. The force was attacked by several thousand troopers. The Kansas regiment receiving the first shock, and giving way, crowded through the lines of the 18th and left it to take up the fight alone. Seven fierce charges were repelled. More than its own numbers were put out of action, but it was finally surrounded when, with fixed bayonets, it cut its way out and reached Camden, having sustained a loss of 77 killed, wounded and missing.

The wretched three weeks' retreat to Little Rock followed, Col. Edwards holding the reserve and guarding the ordnance train at the battle of Jenkins' Ferry. Resuming its duty as garrison at Fort Smith, the regiment moved on numerous minor expeditions and was often compelled to forage to keep from actual starvation, the river below being blockaded. Col. Edwards was promoted to brigadier-general and was succeeded as colonel by Ltc. Campbell. The regiment marched to Fort Gibson in November to meet a supply train from Fort Scott, but, finding it had not arrived, set out on the evening of the 27th with two ears of corn each and one tablespoonful of coffee for each mess of four, as rations, and found the train over 100 miles distant four days later. The regiment passed the winter and spring in alternate starvation and plenty, remaining on garrison duty at Fort Smith until the latter part of the summer of 1865 when it was mustered out. Its original strength was 866; gain by recruits, 9; total, 875.

Santa Maria Cemetery

The Santa Maria Cemetery is located at 730 E. Stowell Road in Santa Maria, CA 93454. Cemetery gates open daily at dawn and close at dusk. Call (805) 925-4595 for more information.

The map depicts the location of Civil War veteran gravesites in the cemetery. This property was considered to be far enough outside of the downtown area that it wouldn't be in the way of planned growth. The town was encroaching on a cemetery that was started in 1872 called the Thornburg-Jones Cemetery. The International Order of Odd Fellows and Free & Accepted Masons Cemetery was started July 9, 1883, by the I.O.O.F. Lodge in conjunction with the Hesperian Lodge, F. & A.M. In 1884 the Thornburg-Jones Cemetery was moved to the new location. Removal of all remains was completed by 1886.

The Santa Maria Cemetery District was established August 6, 1917, in response to a petition by the electors in the District. The Cemetery was organized as a Special District in and for the County of Santa Barbara.

Shaded areas on the map show the locations of veteran's gravesites. More than one veteran may be in a highlighted boundary. There are twelve possible gravesites within each of the numbered area. The numbering system is not easily interpreted. When standing within the cemetery, you may observe plot 66 adjacent to plot 91. This is true because of the way the plots were added. Plots 65 and 92 are across the road in line. It may be necessary to get your bearings as you walk from one gravesite to another. In some cases you may find gravesites adjacent but not in the numerical order expected. It can be quite confusing.

The Santa Maria Woman's Relief Corps circa 1880.

The original cemetery is bordered on the north by Stowell Road and west by College. Stowell Road borders plots numbered 1 to 18. Once you enter the cemetery from College, turn right until you reach the mausoleum area, part of the original grounds. Park safely and get your bearings. Depending on where you park, your walk can begin in any direction. The old flag pole placed by the Women's Relief Corps is a great place to begin.

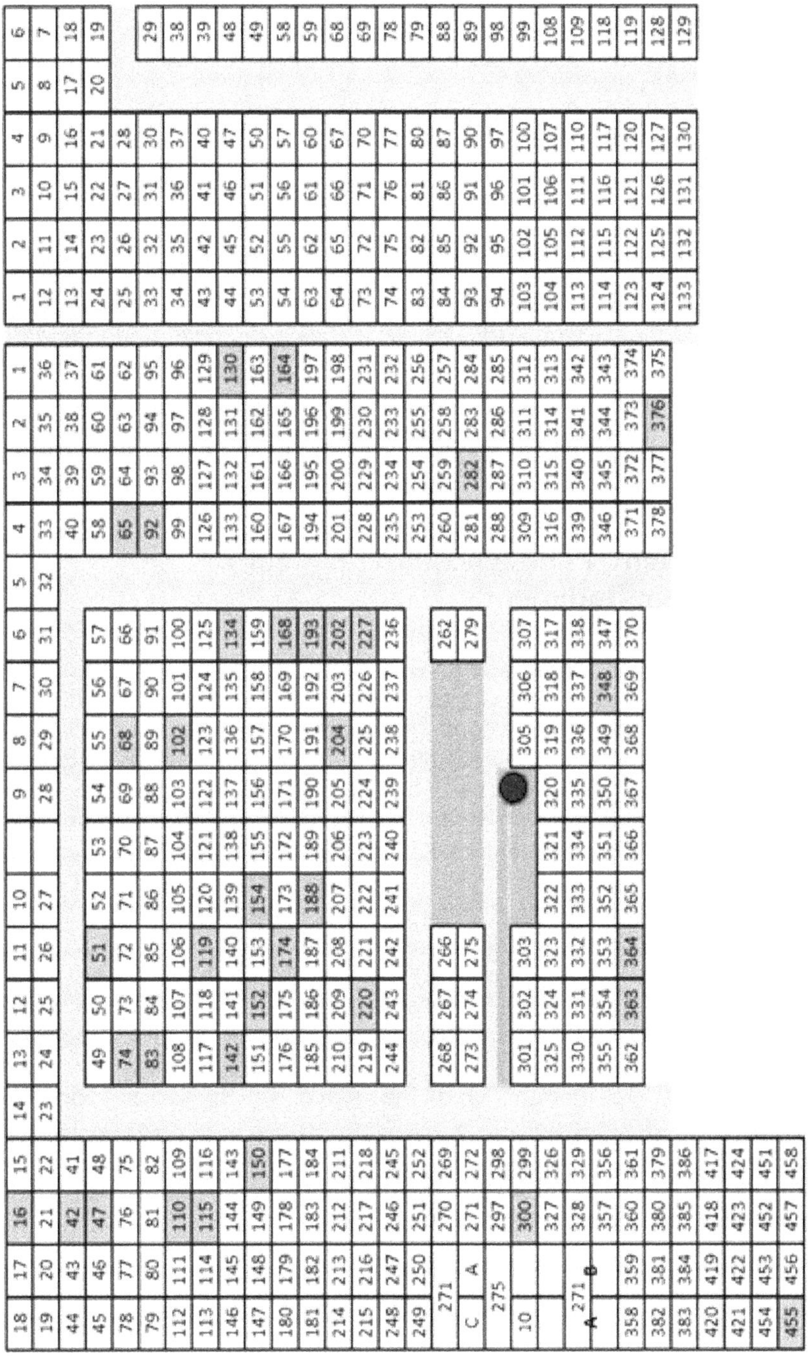

Litzenberg, John P.
Company G, 28th Pennsylvania Infantry Militia
Grave #12   Lot #363
Born: 1864. Died: 1934.

 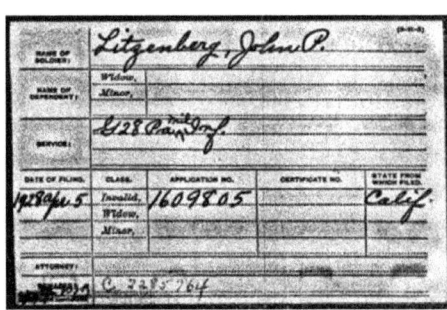

28th Regiment, Pennsylvania Volunteers
'Goldstream Regiment'

Early in June of 1861, John W. Geary obtained permission from President Lincoln to raise, in Pennsylvania, a regiment of volunteers to serve for three years. He accordingly established a camp at Oxford Park, in Philadelphia, and, on the 28th of that month, the Twenty-eighth Regiment, which was uniformed and equipped at his own expense, was mustered into the service of the United States. The regiment, when completed, consisted of fifteen companies, numbering fifteen hundred and fifty-one officers and enlisted men brought together from various sections of the state. Company G was from Allegheny County.

While Colonel Geary was actively engaged in forming, equipping and drilling his regiment, events were transpiring that demanded prompt action on the part of the U.S. Government relative to raising additional troops and hastening them to the field. On July 21st, the disastrous Battle of Bull Run was fought; and the panic which seized upon and disorganized a great portion of the Northern army, spread its terrifying influence through all parts of the Northern States, and had the effect to arouse the heads of the national departments to realize the real danger with which the country was threatened.

Marshall, John Luna
Company C, 46th Iowa Infantry
Grave #12   Lot #202
Born: 1845. Died: 1902.

 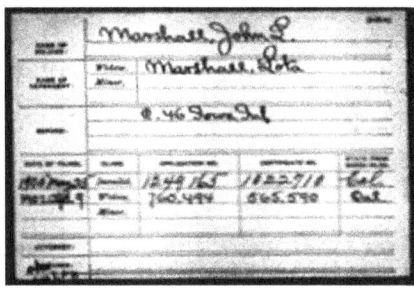

Civil War Dead

The number of American Civil War dead was not matched by the combined toll of other American conflicts until the War in Vietnam. At Gettysburg 51,000 DIED. Most casualties and deaths in the Civil War were the result of non-combat related disease. For every three soldiers killed in battle, five more died of disease. The primitive nature of Civil War medicine, both in its intellectual underpinnings and in its practice in the armies, meant that many wounds and illnesses were unnecessarily fatal. Approximately one-in-four soldiers that went to war never returned home. Of those who returned home, one-in-thirteen Civil War soldiers returned home missing one or more limbs.

The average Civil War soldier was 26 years old, weighed 143 pounds and stood 5' 8" tall (Library of Congress).

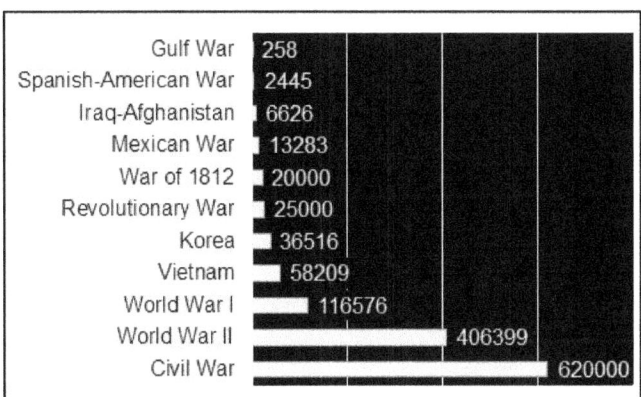

May, John Curtis
Company F, 56th Regiment Illinois Infantry
Grave #3   Lot #204
Born: 1833. Died: 1907.

 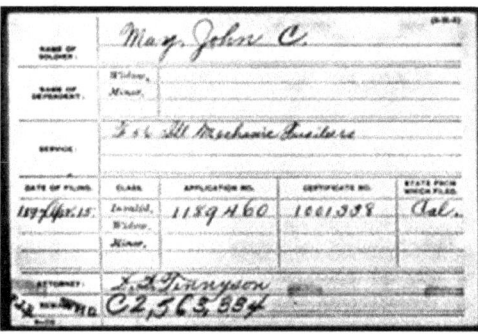

John May mustered in February 27, 1862, to the 56th Illinois Infantry Company F, Mechanic Fusiliers, as a sergeant. He was mustered out August 12, 1865.

Mechanics & Fusiliers Letter

This entry was posted 1st Regiment Mechanics & Fusiliers, Camp Webb.

Oct 27, 61

Dear Sister

I am now a Soldier for the union and liberty I have enlisted in the first regiment of Mechanics Fusiliers Col. I.W. Wilson, Commanding. I was at home about one week and there heard that George had enlisted and was at Washington and I hope that he will do his duty for his Country and home

I want you to write to him and tell him where I am and to write to me tell him to direct to Camp Webb Chigo Illinois, care of Capt. I. Lawson

I will now comence to write to you and hope that this will find you in good health I never so healthey in my life I gained about 18 lbs in about 5 weeks We have just drawn our accounts and we calculate to march about 7 miles tomorrow I have not had any letters from home yet and I dont calculate to write any more until I get an answer from some of them no more at pressent from your

Affectionate
Brother
G.E. Portman

Mead, Giles Ward
Company B, 7th Iowa Infantry
Grave #12   Lot #16
Born: April 9, 1838. Died: January 27, 1913.

Giles Ward Mead was born in Summit County, Ohio, on April 9, 1838, of a New England family. He accompanied his father, Daniel B. Mead, to Michigan. In Rock Grove Township in 1854 his father organized the first Baptist church, of which Giles became a member. At the first meeting in Rock Grove Township to call for army volunteers, Giles W. Mead was the first man to offer his life to save the Union. He enlisted at Charles City in Company B, 7th Iowa Volunteer Infantry. He was promoted from corporal to first lieutenant, fought in 19 battles and marched with Sherman to the sea. He was one of the last to apply for a pension, opposing the urgency of his friends in this matter by saying that he would not ask help as long as he could help himself. He had great faith in God and reverence for His word. "I am the resurrection, Earth and sky. A Savior sing. What victory hath the grave today, And death what sting!" Lieut. Giles Mead died at Nipomo, California, on Jan. 27, 1913. The cause of his death was paralysis.

Moore, Oliver Perry
Company E, 11th Indiana Cavalry
Grave #10   Lot #282
Born: August 1, 1849. Died: January 14, 1922.

Old Soldiers Home

The National Asylum for Disabled Volunteer Soldiers and Sailors of the Civil War was incorporated in 1865 when Congress passed legislation in support of these veterans. Volunteers were not eligible for care in the existing regular army and navy home facilities. This legislation, one of the last acts signed by President Lincoln, marked the entrance of the United States into the direct provision of care for the temporary versus career military. The Asylum was renamed the National Home for Disabled Volunteer Soldiers (NHDVS) in 1873. It was also known as the Old Soldiers Home. Between 1867 and 1929, the Home expanded to ten branches and one sanatorium. The **Sawtelle Veterans Home** was a care home for disabled American veterans in what is today part of the Los Angeles metropolitan area. The home, formally the Pacific Branch of the National Home for Disabled Volunteer Soldiers, was established in 1887 on 300 acres of Rancho San Vicente y Santa Monica lands donated by Senator John P. Jones and Arcadia B. de Baker. The following year, the site grew by an additional 200 acres; in 1890, 20 acres more were appended for use as a veterans cemetery. With more than 1,000 veterans in residence, a new hospital was erected in 1900. This hospital was replaced in 1927 by the Wadsworth Hospital.

16107 Oliver P. Moore

MILITARY HISTORY

Time and Place of Each Enlistment	Rank	Company and Regiment	Time and Place of Discharge	Cause of Discharge	Disabilities When Admitted to the Home
Dec. 29, 1863	Pr.	E 9 Ind Cav.	20 May 1865 Medina - Ind Pmate	Dis.	Chron Colitis + Mus Rheumatism Intestinal Stasis Neurmurus

DOMESTIC HISTORY

Where Born	Age	Height	Complexion	Color of Eyes	Color of Hair	Read and Write	Religion	Occupation	Residence Subsequent to Discharge	Married or Single	Name and Address of Nearest Relative
Indiana	70	5.10	Light	Gray	Gray	Yes	Prot.	Farmer	Santa Maria Calif.	Wid.	Mrs Hamel Cash Santa Maria Calif

HOME HISTORY

Rate of Pension	Date of Admission, Re-Admission and Transfer	Conditions of Re-Admission	Date of Discharge and Transfer	Cause of Discharge	Date of Death	Cause of Death
30/30 3 July 20, 1921	Ad. GB Aug 9. 1919.				Jan 15-1922	Chr Intestinal nephritis Hemiplegia

GENERAL REMARKS

PAPERS		Location of Grave and Remarks
Admission Paper	1	Body removed
Army Discharges		
Certificate of Service	1	
Pension Certificate	2270	
EFFECTS		
Cash A.S. Appraised at $150.00	$	
Pension Money	none	$
Personal, Appraised at	6.10 sold $	
Total	$	

How Disposed of To Mrs. Sallie Warren, administratix 304 East Main St % Hopkins Hotel. Santa Maria Calif.

Morgan, Thomas L.
Company I, 28th Iowa Infantry
Grave #6   Lot #68
Born: September 29, 1837. Died: June 11, 1887.

Iowa

Iowa was not a location of any significant battles during the Civil War. It did send large supplies of food to the armies and the eastern cities. 76,242 Iowa men (out of a total population of 674,913 in 1860) served in the military, many in combat units attached to the western armies. 13,001 died of wounds or disease. 8,500 Iowa men were wounded. Cemeteries throughout the South contain the remains of Iowa soldiers who fell during the Civil War, with the largest concentration at Vicksburg National Cemetery. A number also died in Confederate prison camps, including Andersonville prison. Though the total number of Iowans who served in the military during the Civil War seems small compared to the more heavily populated eastern and southern states, no other state, north or south, had a higher percentage of its male population between the ages of 15 and 40 serve in the military during the course of the war.

Iowa contributed 48 regiments of state infantry, 1 regiment of black infantry (the 1st Iowa Volunteer Infantry Regiment (African Descent)), 9 regiments of cavalry, and 4 artillery batteries.

Paulding, Ormond Pinkerton
Company A, 69th Ohio Infantry
Grave #6   Lot #193
Born: September 13, 1845. Died: October 21, 1933.

Ormond Paulding was born in Turkey in 1845. He enlisted at the age of 17 as a private in Company A, Ohio 69th Infantry Regiment on February 26 1864. He was mustered out on July 17, 1865, at Louisville, KY.

Dr. Ormond Pinkerton Paulding was the last surviving member of Foote Post, G.A.R.. He was a member of Sherman's army in the Civil War during the historic march from Atlanta to Savannah, Sherman's March to the Sea. Serving also in World War I, he enrolled in the medical corps. He graduated from the College of Medicine, University of Michigan, in 1875. He arrived in Santa Maria in 1892.

Powell, William Vaughn
Company I, Field & Staff, 99th Indiana Infantry
Grave #8   Lot #102
Born: May 22, 1826. Died: August 26, 1903.

During the Civil War William Powell enlisted as a captain at Peru, Miami County, Indiana, on October 10, 1862, and was commissioned commander of Company I, 99th Indiana Infantry, on October 25. Captain Powell was promoted to Major on May 1, 1865, brevetted (increase in rank without increase in pay, often granted as an honor) a Lieutenant Colonel on May 2, and transferred to Field & Staff, 99th Indiana Infantry, on May 20, 1865. Lieutenant-Colonel Powell was mustered out at Washington, D.C., on June 5, 1865. After the war he returned to his family at Jefferson, where he remained until at least 1867. He had moved to California and settled at Willits, Mendocino County, by 1874. He was living at Little Lake, Mendocino County, by 1880 (1880 US Census). William later moved his family to Santa Maria, Santa Barbara County, where he remained until he died. William was a member Santa Maria's Admiral Foote Post, No. 89, Grand Army of the Republic (G.A.R.).

Pritchard, Adolph
Company F, 3rd Regiment, North Carolina Mountain Infantry
Grave #9   Lot #364
Born: April 17, 1847. Died: September 10, 1922.

North Carolina Mountain Infantry

Company F, 3rd Regiment, North Carolina Mountain Infantry was organized at Knoxville, Tennessee, June, 1864. It served as a scouting unit and on patrol duty around Knoxville, Tennessee, and in East Tennessee until December, 1864. Scouting from Morristown, Tennessee, into North Carolina from June 13 to July 15, 1864. Mustered out August 8, 1865.

The 3rd North Carolina Mountain Infantry was an all-volunteer mounted infantry regiment that served in the Union Army. The regiment was predominantly composed of Union Loyalists from North Carolina and Tennessee but also included volunteers from several other Southern states.

Under the command of Colonel George Washington Kirk, it became associated with unconventional and guerrilla-like tactics. Consequently the regiment became known as Kirk's Raiders, and the men were labeled bushwhackers or, more generously, as mountaineers because the majority of the men hailed from the Blue Ridge Mountains of Western North Carolina and East Tennessee.

Robinson, Alfred Wesley "Alfredo"
Sergeant, Company H, 16th Kansas Cavalry
Grave #9   Lot #47
Born: 1842. Died: November 12, 1909.

Union Civil War Veterans Headstones

There are specific styles of upright marble headstones to mark the graves of Civil War Union soldiers. Inscribed in raised lettering inside a recessed shield, these recessed-shield headstones are available in three marble sizes or one granite size: 12" wide, 3" thick, and 42" high; 13" wide, 3" thick and 42" high; and 10" wide, 3" thick and 39" high.

The inscription on the recessed-shield headstone is limited. For Civil War Union, a shield is inscribed that encompasses the arched name and abbreviated military organization. Because of the special design and historical uniform significance, no emblem of belief or additional inscription may be inscribed. The dates of birth and death are inscribed below the shield.

Stilwell, William Wilson
Company D, 16th Missouri State Militia Calvary
Grave #11   Lot #168
Born: 1842. Died: November 12, 1909.

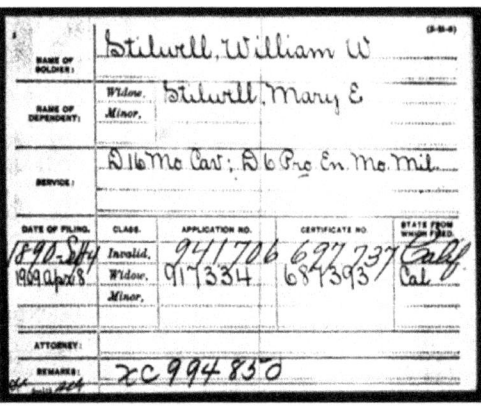

William Stilwell was living in Marshall County, Tennessee, in November 1850 (1850 US Census). During the Civil War he enlisted as a private and was mustered into Company D, 16th Missouri State Militia Cavalry. He married Mary Elizabeth Florence in Webster County, Missouri, December 20, 1864. After the war he moved to California where he became a farmer outside Santa Maria by 1880 (1880 US Census). William was a member of Santa Maria's Foote Post, No. 89, Grand Army of the Republic (G.A.R.). He filed for a Civil War veteran's pension at Santa Maria on September 4, 1890, and received application No. 941,706 and certificate No. 697,737. After his death Mary filed for a Civil War widow's pension at Santa Maria April 8, 1909, and received application No. 917,334 and certificate No. 687,393.

Silva, Antonio Nunes
1st Battalion, California Native Cavalry
Grave #1   Lot #313
Born: 1836. Died: November 15, 1919.

These documents verify enlistment and give details of service.

Stowe, Robert G.
Company F, 112th Illinois Infantry
Grave #9   Lot #152
Born: 1840. Died: May 19, 1921.

 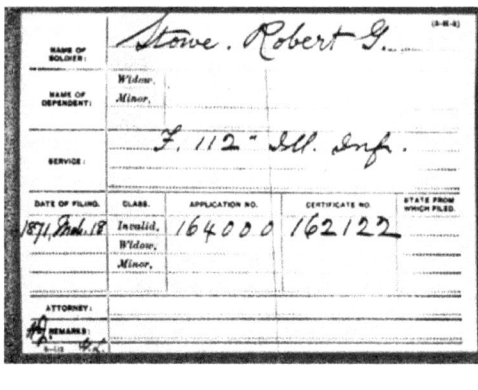

Robert Gilbert Stowe was born in Illinois in 1840. Much can be learned from his military headstone application.

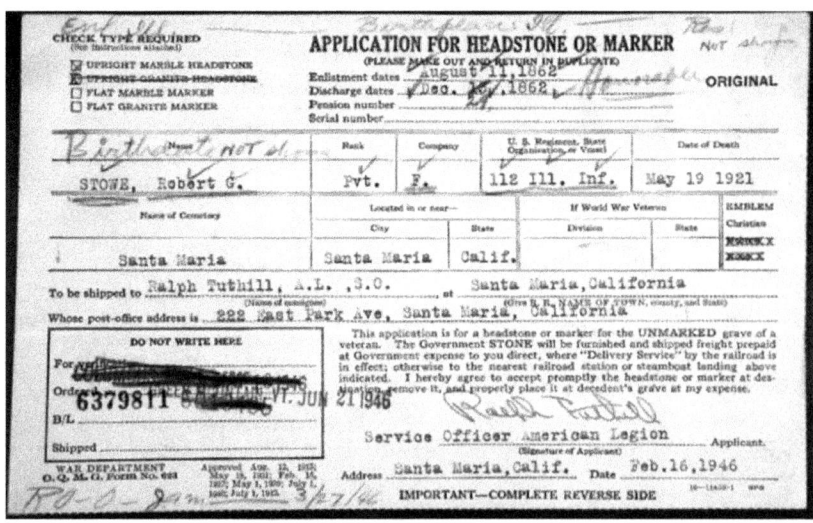

Thornburgh, Jesse H.
Company H, 39th Regiment, Iowa Infantry (Drummer)
Buried in the Mausoleum at the Santa Maria Cemetery
Born: 1839. Died: 1913.

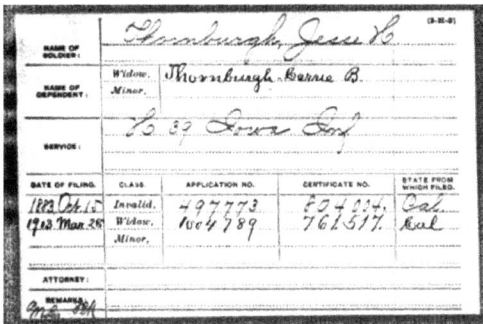

Drummer Boy

The Civil War is sometimes called "The Boys' War," because so many soldiers who fought in it were still in their teens. The rule in the Union Army was that soldiers had to be 18 to join, but many younger boys pretended to be 18.

Often the youngest boys served as drummers. They did a very important job during the Civil War. In the noise and confusion of battle, it was often impossible to hear the officers' orders, so each order was given a series of drumbeats. Both soldiers and drummers had to learn which drumroll meant "meet here" and which meant "attack now" and which meant "retreat," along with all the other commands of the battlefield and camp. The use of drums declined rapidly as the bugle replaced the drum in the signaling role.

When the drummer boys weren't needed for sounding the calls, they were stretcher bearers. They walked around the battlefield looking for the wounded and brought them to medical care.

Thornburgh, Joseph W.
39th Regiment, Iowa Volunteer Infantry
Grave #12   Lot #119
Born: October 16, 1844. Died: June 4, 1873.

Joseph and Jesse Thornburgh were sons of founding Santa Maria "Father" John Thornburgh, who generously donated 40 acres of land along with three others to create Santa Maria, CA. John lost a third son, Henry, named after his own twin brother, during the Civil War. Joseph died young and his early departure is attributed to his service years.

Van Order, George
Company D, 143 New York Infantry
Grave #9   Lot #115
Born: 1843. Died: October 28, 1914.

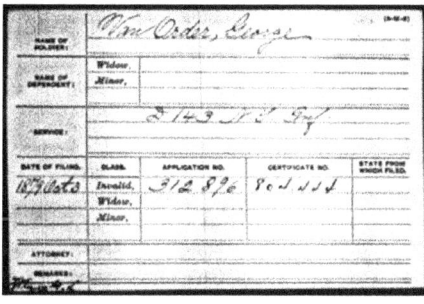

Willson, M. Sibley
Sergeant (Rank out: Corporal)
Company E, 12th Illinois Calvary
Company F, 8th U.S. Veterans Volunteer Infantry
Grave #5   Lot #150
Born: July 15, 1833. Died: February 14, 1916.

Goober Peas: A Confederate Campfire Song

Sitting by the roadside on a summer's day
Chatting with my mess-mates, passing time away
Lying in the shadow underneath the trees
Goodness, how delicious, eating goober peas.
Peas, peas, peas, peas
Eating goober peas
Goodness, how delicious,
Eating goober peas.
Peas, peas, peas, peas
Eating goober peas
Goodness, how delicious,
Eating goober peas.

Just before the battle, the General hears a row
He says "The Yanks are coming, I hear their rifles now."
He turns around in wonder, and what d'ya think he sees?
The Georgia Militia, eating goober peas.
Peas, peas, peas, peas
Eating goober peas
Goodness, how delicious,
Eating goober peas.
Peas, peas, peas, peas
Eating goober peas
Goodness, how delicious,
Eating goober peas.

Wilson, Joseph Henry
U.S. Navy Civil War
Grave #6   Lot #42
Born: 1839. Died: 1911.

 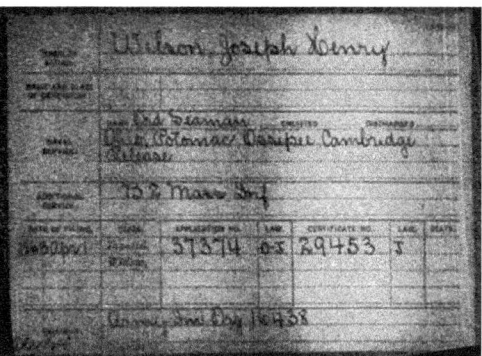

U. S. Navy in the Civil War

At the beginning of the Civil War, the Navy was composed of approximately 90 ships, only around 40 of which were close to combat-capable. The "Anaconda Plan" called for a stiff blockade of Southern seaports in conjunction with an amphibious advance along the line of the Mississippi River. The central demand of the Anaconda Plan, a blockade roughly 3,000 miles in length, was way beyond what the Navy was able to provide. Old ships were filled with stones and sunk in blocking positions around Southern harbors to buy time for the engineers rushing to create a new fleet of warships. Hundreds of civilian ships were pressed into service. Passenger ferries, their sturdy decks built to hold horse carriages, adapted especially well to their new role as river gunboats. The Union navy grew to comprise more than six hundred ships by 1865, the largest in the world at that time, giving the Northern Navy a consistent advantage in the war on the water.

Yelkin, Riner
2nd Independent Battery, Company G, Kansas Cavalry
Light Artillery (Hopkins')
POW
Grave #11   Lot #65
Born: 1839. Died: 1911.

Andersonville Prison

Andersonville held more prisoners at any given time than any of the other Confederate military prisons. It was built in early 1864 after Confederate officials decided to move the large number of Federal prisoners in and around Richmond to a place of greater security and more food. During the 14 months that it existed, more than 45,000 Union soldiers were confined at Andersonville. Almost 13,000 soldiers died from disease, poor sanitation, malnutrition, overcrowding, or exposure.

Civil War Generals Killed by "Friendly Fire"

Most of us are familiar with the term friendly fire. This simply denotes an accident that occurred which resulted in the death of someone on the same side of the battle as the one who brought about that death.

The American Civil War had its share of friendly fire incidents and, in fact, five Civil War generals were killed by friendly fire during some of the most ferocious battles of the war.

It is not something that anyone wishes to happen, but in the heat of battle, accidents happen. No war waged is without friendly fire incidences. Character is always tested on these occasions, as guilt, fault, responsibility, and avoidability are all being placed, borne, and labeled.

1. General Jesse Reno was a Union general and was killed in the Battle of South Mountain.
2. General Thomas Williams was a Union general and was killed in the Battle of Baton Rouge.
3. General Thomas J. "Stonewall" Jackson was a Confederate general and was killed in the Battle of Chancellorsville.
4. General Albert Sidney Johnson was a Confederate general and was killed in the Battle of Shiloh.
5. General Micah Jenkins was a Confederate general and was killed in the Battle of Wilderness.

Veterans

of

The Confederate States of America

The last Confederate veteran,
John Salling,
died in 1958 at age 112.

Lion of Lucerne: Oakland Cemetery, Atlanta, GA

Established in 1850, the Oakland Cemetery in Atlanta, has 6,900 Confederates buried in its grounds, including five generals. It is Atlanta's oldest cemetery. The first soldiers were buried as early as September 1863, following the Battle of Chickamauga. Soldiers who died in Atlanta while seeking treatment for wounds or disease were also buried there before the Battle of Atlanta in July 1864. During the Battle of Atlanta, Union soldiers vandalized the cemetery. They stole nameplates, broke into crypts, and exhumed Confederate dead in order to use the coffins for Union corpses. Wooden markers in the cemetery were replaced by marble ones in 1890.

Based on the "Lion of Lucerne" in Switzerland, the memorial of a mortally wounded lion lying on a Confederate flag was erected in the Confederate section of the Oakland Cemetery in 1894. It was carved from a single block of Georgia marble, the largest block of marble ever quarried up to that time.

Woman's Relief Corps

This headstone belongs to Patrick Bartron's wife and is located next to his gravesite at Grave #10, Lot 51. Her name is Alsia Anna Dodge Bartron. Her brother was also a veteran, his name was Rinaldo Dodge.

Recognized in 1883, the Woman's Relief Corps (W.R.C.) was the official woman's auxiliary to the Grand Army of the Republic. The W.R.C. was one of many women's organizations that were founded after the American Civil War. In 1879 a group of Massachusetts women began a secret organization, and its members were women who were loyal to the North during the Civil War. It didn't matter where the applicants lived during the Civil War as long as they could prove they were loyal to the Union. While one might assume that this organization was only for white women, there were many posts across the country that had Black American women as members. The only challenge identifying these women is that the Woman's Relief Corps records do not often specify the races of its membership. The organization was designed to assist the G.A.R., promote and help run Memorial Day, petition the federal government for nurses' pensions, and promote true allegiance to the United States of America and teach patriotism and love of country.

Woman's Relief Corps Medal

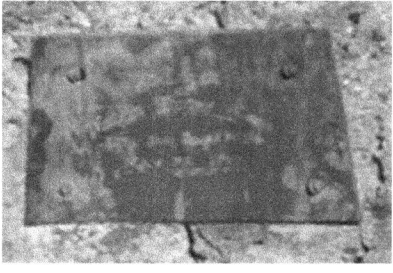

This Woman's Relief Corps Plaque is located on the flagpole which is in front of the mausoleum at the Santa Maria Cemetery.

Haydon, John Harrison
6th Regiment, Kentucky Cavalry
Grave #11   Lot #74
Born: 1837. Died: 1931.

Confederate Pension Act

The Confederate Pension Act was passed by the Kentucky General Assembly in March 1912 to provide aid to indigent and disabled Confederate veterans of the Civil War and their widows. Any Confederate veteran or widow of a veteran living in Kentucky in 1912 or after could apply for a pension, regardless of the state in which he resided or the unit in which he served during the war. Pensions for Union veterans were funded by the federal government.

The Southern Cross of Honor

The inscription on the special style for Civil War Confederate headstones is limited. The Southern Cross of Honor is automatically inscribed at the top. The name is arched, followed by abbreviated military organization and dates of birth and death. No additional items can be inscribed. If a flat marker is desired for a Confederate soldier, the Southern Cross of Honor can be inscribed if requested, or any one of other approved emblems may be inscribed if requested.

Lawrence, William S.
Camp of Instruction, Talladega, Alabama
No headstone
Grave #3   Lot #150
Born: 1838. Died: 1934.

Camp of Instruction

In April of 1862 the Confederate government established two camps of instruction in Alabama. These were Camp Watts at Notasulga (Camp of Instruction No. 1) and Camp Buckner at Talladega (Camp of Instruction No. 2). These camps were established for collecting recruits. Faced with a serious manpower shortage, a compulsory military service law (draft) went into effect in April 1862. Men between the ages of 18 and 35 would be obligated to enroll for service. Talladega and Notasulga were selected as camp sites to collect recruits, which had been volunteers up to this time. Enrollees were eventually assigned to a front-line unit.

Miles, William T.
30th Battalion, Virginia Sharpshooters
Grave #5   Lot #142
Born: August 16, 1839. Died: July 16, 1896.

Virginia Sharpshooters

The 30th Battalion, Virginia Sharpshooters was created in 1862 from the remains of three artillery batteries with the addition of three further companies made up of transfers. Companies A and B were composed of men from Captain Stephen Adams' Gauley Artillery and Captain Napoleon B. French's Battery. Both units served under General John B. Floyd from the beginning of the war until surrendering at Battle of Fort Donelson.

Fort Donelson

Fort Donelson was a fortress built by the Confederacy during the American Civil War to control the Cumberland River leading to the heart of Tennessee and the heart of the Confederacy. The fort was named after Confederate General Daniel S. Donelson.

Miller, George A.
Company E, 2nd Battalion Alabama Light Artillery
Grave #8   Lot #455
Born: August 12, 1834. Died: January 14, 1936.

2nd Battalion Alabama Light Artillery

The 2nd Alabama Light Artillery Battalion, Company E, was formed at Mobile in January 1862. It was attached to the Department of the Gulf, and after January, 1864, the Department of Alabama, Mississippi, and East Louisiana. The unit was stationed at or near Mobile throughout the war and participated in the conflicts at Forts Gaines and Morgan, Spanish Fort, and Fort Blakely. It surrendered on 4 May 1865.

Grand Army of the Republic

The "Grand Army of the Republic" (G.A.R.) was a fraternal organization composed of veterans of the Union Army, Union Navy, Marines and the U.S. Revenue Cutter Service who served in the American Civil War for the northern forces. Founded in 1866 in Decatur, Illinois, and growing to include hundreds of posts across the nation, it was dissolved in 1956 when its last member, Albert Woolson (1847–1956), of Duluth, Minnesota, died at age 109.

Linking men through their experience of the war, the G.A.R. became among the first organized advocacy groups in American politics, supporting voting rights for black veterans, promoting patriotic education, helping to make Memorial Day a national holiday, lobbying the United States Congress to establish regular veterans' pensions, and supporting Republican political candidates. Its peak membership, at more than 490,000, was in 1890. It was succeeded by the Sons of Union Veterans of the Civil War (S.U.V.C.W.), composed of male descendants of Union Army and Navy veterans.

Foote Post No. 89, G.A.R. Santa Maria

The following is a record of the men who were listed as the founding members of the Grand Army of the Republic (G.A.R.), Foote Post No. 89, in Santa Maria. Some of these veterans are presented in the preceding pages. Many of these men passed through Santa Maria to another final resting place. All of these men lived and were part of the G.A.R. in Santa Maria in 1886.

Officers: 1886

Morton, L.K.	**Commander:**	
	Company I, Pennsylvania Bucktails	
	Company F, Veterans Reserve	
Powell, W.V.	**Senior Vice-Commander**	
	Company H, 99th Indiana Infantry	
Elliott, Jas.	**Junior Vice-Commander**	
	Company A, 46th New York Infantry	
Ayres, W.W.	**Adjutant**	
	Company K, 39th Missouri Infantry	
Bell, B.F.	**Quartermaster**	
	Company A, 11th Pennsylvania Infantry	
Bartron, H.	**Surgeon**	
	Company E, 149th Pennsylvania Infantry	
Kelsey, D.N.	**Chaplain**	
	Company E, 1st Massachusetts Battalion	
Kincaid, O.D.	**Officer of the Day**	
	Company A, 1st Iowa Cavalry	
Whitford, M.	**Officer of the Guard**	
	Company G, 2d California Cavalry	
Field, F.F.	**Sergeant Major**	
	Company E, 15th Connecticut Infantry	
Moran, Thos.	**Quartermaster Sergeant**	
	Company B 34th Wisconsin Infantry	

General Membership

Foster, David	Company C, Kansas Cavalry
Gale, S.M.	Company K, 2d Missouri Infantry
Goudy, G.M.	Company F, 7th California Infantry
Montgomery, D.C.	Company D, 17th Ohio Infantry
Smith, John	Company D, 2d Connecticut Infantry
Stilwell, W.W.	16th Missouri Infantry
Van Husen, H.S.	Company C, 9th Minnesota Infantry & Company C, 67th U.S. Colored Infantry
Winters, Nathaniel F.	Company C, California Cavalry
Yelkin, R.	2d & 9th Kansas Cavalry

Bibliography

The following websites and organizations were used extensively in the creation of this book. It is not possible to cite specific sources as they were used in this work because most articles are a combination of material from multiple sources. This bibliography merely recognizes the work performed by others without which this volume would not have been possible.

alabamagenealogy.org
Ancestry.com (Genealogy website)
archives.gov (National Archives: Civil War Records)
civilwar.org (Civil War Trust website)
civilwarsoldiersearch.com (Guide to Civil War research resources)
FamilySearch.com (Genealogy website of The Church of Jesus Christ of
    Latter-day Saints)
findagrave.com (Graveyard website)
go.fold3.com (Fold3-U.S. Military Records)
kvm.kvcc.edu/civilwar/tag/1st-regiment-mechanics-fusiliers/
nationalparkservice.org (U. S. National Park Service)
thecivilwaromnibus.com (articles exploring the Civil War)
wikipedia.org (Wikipedia, on-line encyclopedia)

Santa Maria Cemetery District
Santa Maria Times
Santa Maria Valley Historical Society

United States Census: 1850, 1860, 1880, 1900 and 1910

Anonymous. *The Union Army: A History of Military Affairs in the Loyal
    States, 1861-65 -- Records of the Regiments in the Union Army
    – Cyclopedia of Battles – Memoirs of Commanders and Soldiers.*
    Volume 4. Madison, WI: Federal Publishing Company, 1908.
    Reprint. Nabu Press, 2010.

Acknowledgements

The Santa Maria Valley Historical Society and the author wish to thank the following for their contributions to this book. In the final analysis, they are the ones who made in happen.

Edward J. Zemaitis; President, Board of Directors
                      Santa Maria Valley Historical Society/Museum

Gordon Smith, findagrave.com contributor, provided a number of additional photographs

Santa Barbara Foundation

www.ingramcontent.com/pod-product-compliance
Lightning Source LLC
Chambersburg PA
CBHW070629050426
42450CB00011B/3154